make your day

handmade
wedding

creative craft projects
to personlize your big day

Kim Wilson Byers

LEISURE ARTS, INC. • Maumelle, Arkansas

A Note
From Kim

I was married in the gardens of a historic antebellum home, nestled on a high river bank, in Alabama a few, or more, years ago. The first reason I chose this venue was of course that it was amazingly beautiful, and the second, it only cost $85 to rent it for the day. I, probably like you, wanted a lovely wedding, but I didn't see a need to spend a fortune.

I was married in early April and not many flowers were blooming yet. So instead of hiring our florist to make more arrangements for the garden area, my mom, who was seeing to almost every detail already, planted flowers in the garden the day before the wedding. Yes, she did ask permission of the groundkeepers!

2

I'd love for you to join me at TheCelebrationShoppe.com/HandmadeWedding for more wedding craft ideas and templates, including projects in my Cricut wedding cartridge.

My grandmother, who took precious time away from caring for her disabled daughter to help me select the most beautiful wedding dress, also took it in for me to make sure it was a perfect fit. My mom's best friend, a true southern belle, kept everyone focused, perfectly pressed and on schedule on my big day. She even packed our going away picnic for the honeymoon, which of course we accidentally left behind at the hotel. And last, but never least, my dad not only walked me down the aisle, but made me laugh and not trip on the cobblestones, while we did!

I dedicate this book to my amazing family and friends for helping me have the wedding I dreamed of, with style and grace, and for much less than if I had paid someone else to do it all!

My hope is that ideas within these pages will inspire you to craft your own beautiful wedding day too. Not perfect. Perfect is overrated. Enjoy your day, and take any hiccups in stride. It will give you something to laugh about on your anniversaries!

m kim

you're engaged!

So he popped the question.
Congratulations!

Now the fun begins.
Some say the stress begins,
but it doesn't have to be that
way. Plan ahead, create and
craft as you go, and enjoy every
single minute of it. After all,
you are planning for one of the
happiest days of your life!

congratulatio

I'm so thrilled to be sharing some easy DIY projects to help you personalize your day. I hope you find something lovely to create, or the inspiration to make something all your own, within these pages.

contents

Getting Started

Ask Your Bridesmaids

Say I Do

Reception

Send Off

getting started

First Things First

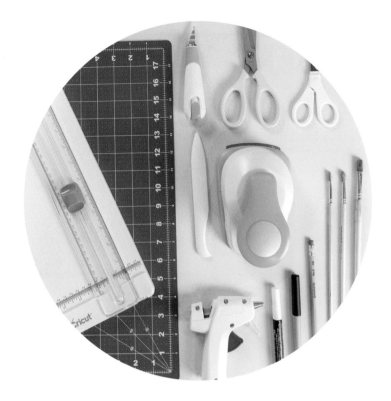

Pick a color palette and choose your
tools to make your day!

Decisions, decisions! Before the big day arrives, you'll make many, many

decisions – from the wedding venue, to the cake style and flavor, to the

seating arrangements at the reception. Use this book to decide which

items you'll create to make your special day beautifully handmade.

[pick your own color palette]

Well, you're getting married! Now that the excitement has settled in, you need to get started making decisions.

10

First on that list is choosing your color palette. It will set the stage for almost every decision you make for the next several months, from bridesmaid dresses, to florals, to table linens.

When choosing a color palette, be inspired by the wedding setting itself, the season in which you are exchanging vows, your favorite colors in your wardrobe or home décor, or colors that just make you happy!

You can choose from 2-5 colors; if you choose 4 or more, be sure 2 of the colors are more neutral or go with tonal shades of a color. Colors can be soft pastels, vibrant brights, calming neutrals, or anything in between.

Do try to avoid the latest and greatest fad colors as the main colors; you want your photos and memories to withstand the test of time. Those special hues make great accents in small doses.

Bold, saturated hues work well for summer weddings, while silvery tones are lovely for winter weddings.

Once you have a palette, start collecting supplies in your colors. And if you love something, but it's the wrong color, get it anyway and paint it.

color palette

[gather the right tools]

Do not make a craft harder than it should be. Buy the right tool for the job. It will save your craft supplies, and it will save your sanity.

Here are a few of my favorites and why:

- Straight edge cutter – helps me cut perfect lines. Instead of jagged edges or uneven shapes, I have neat, clean-cut designs for crafting.

- Clear ruler – necessary for measuring and keeping crafts symmetrical, of course, but I find it extremely helpful to see the material underneath when crafting.

- Scissors – detail scissors and regular are both important. I use small detail scissors for the intricate paper cuts and ribbon. I use my regular scissors for everything else except fabric. I have a separate pair of scissors and a rotary cutter for fabric only. Paper will dull your blades over time.

12

- Self-healing mat – it's not only a great cutting surface, but it protects my crafting surface from other things.

- Craft knife – it gets in all the small places that detail scissors can't. Also great for thick materials.

- Clear fishing line – strong and invisible. I use it for everything from hanging balloons to fastening flowers to wreaths.

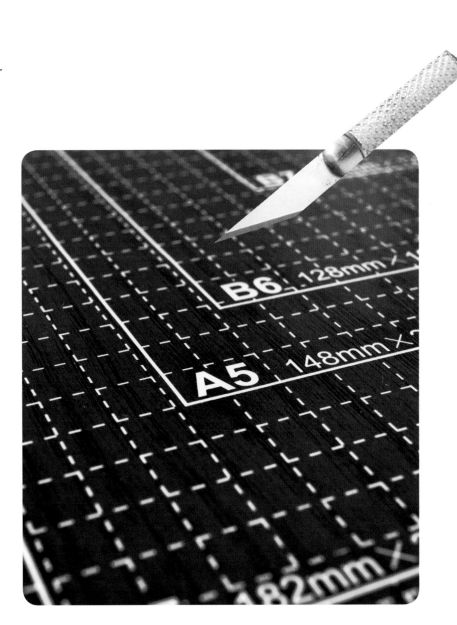

tools

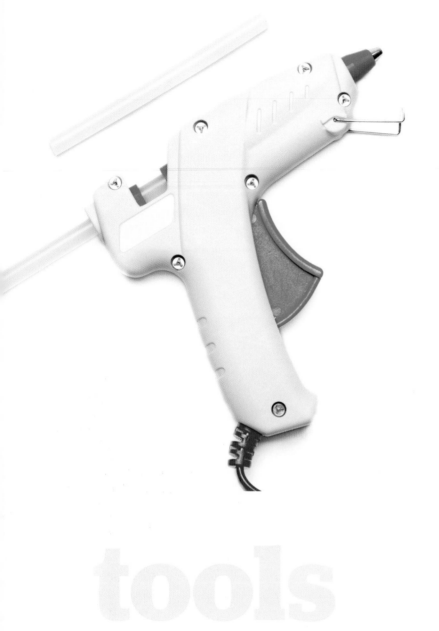

tools

- Hot glue gun – a favorite for me. Adhering to most surfaces, I use hot glue when I want a craft to stick fast.

- Adhesive dots – perfect for paper projects, but I also use them for things that I want to stick for a minute or two while I work. Unless the box states permanent, most surfaces will release the dot with no mess.

- Bone folder – this tool gives me the perfect crease every time when paper crafting.

14

- Paintbrushes – not only great for painting, but they can be great for clean-up. Brushing away stray fibers when dry and washing away small mishaps on chalkboards when wet.

- Chalk marker – easier to use than chalk sticks and writes on more surfaces than just chalkboards.

- Pencil – no explanation necessary, right! I'm a note taker and mark maker. I like things in line.

He popped the question!

He popped the question! Will you help me
tie the knot?

You're asking your best friends to stand next to you on one of the biggest
days in your life. You're asking them to give you the gift of their time and
their money. Make the "ask" something special that they will remember!
And candidly, can't say no to!

[bridesmaid invitation]

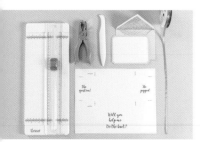

Supplies

- Notecards in your wedding colors, with envelopes
- White cardstock
- Ribbon
- Adhesive dots

Tools

- Straight edge cutter with cutting blade and scoring blade
- Bone folder
- Hole punch

STEPS

1 Gather Supplies Shop the stationery aisle for notecards. This design fits standard size notecards, approximately 4¼" x 5½". For the hole punch, small round or small square works great. For the ribbon, choose something that is soft, doesn't have wire, and not a heavy grosgrain. Those ribbons might tear the cardstock when you thread it through. Photocopy the designs on pages 88-89 onto white cardstock for as many invitations that you need.

These sweet little cards couldn't be easier!

2 Score Use the guides at the top and bottom of the card band to score each vertical line. This will allow you to easily fold the card band.

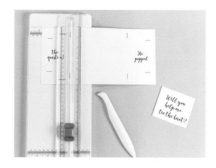

3 Trim Using a straight edge cutter, trim the card band into a strip. For the inside message card, trim to fit the notecard.

Don't stop here. The invitation is darling, but pair it with a gift box of goodies!

4 Assemble Fold the card band at each scored line. Use the hole punch to punch a small hole on either side of the flap. Thread ribbon through the holes. Use an adhesive dot to attach the message card to the front of the notecard. Slip the notecard inside the card band, fold over the ends, and tie the ribbon.

Will you
help me
tie the knot?

[graphic tees]

Make a graphic tee that makes a statement!

Part of the fun of getting married is telling everyone, or in this case, showing everyone. These tees are perfect for everything from shopping sprees, to the bachelorette party, to the morning of. I chose to paint these as if they are a bit worn, but with a second coat of paint, the letters will be solid and crisp. Other popular graphics are "Bride To Be," "Getting Hitched," and "Future Mrs." These are so easy to make, you'll want to make them for your entire bridal party!

Supplies

- T-shirt
- Freezer paper
- Fabric paint

Tools

- Heavy duty detail craft knife
- Ruler
- Self-healing cutting mat
- Iron
- Ironing pad
- Tape
- Foam paintbrush
- Paint palette or paper plate
- Cardboard

ask your
bridesmaids

STEPS

1 Gather Supplies You'll need all the tools listed on page 20. For the supplies, make sure you purchase freezer paper. Parchment paper and wax paper will not work. You need a coated surface and an uncoated surface, which is what freezer paper has. One side sticks to the fabric and the other is clean so it doesn't damage your iron.

2 Select Design & Cut The #BrideTribe design can be used multiple ways. Just cut out only the pieces you want.

Copy the template on page 87. Tape it to the self-healing mat. Cover the template with freezer paper, placing the paper shiny side down. Using the craft knife, cut out the design. I recomment going over the design corners twice being careful not to press too hard. The paper cuts easily, so the second pass is to make sure all the fine corners are cut, allowing the excess paper to be easily removed.

Use a ruler when cutting the straight sides of letters to help keep the knife straight and have a perfect cut.

3 Apply & Iron Measure the shirt and center the design. Using a medium heat iron, with steam turned off, iron the freezer paper to the shirt. For letters like "D" that have center areas, iron the large pieces on first, and then fill in the smaller elements.

tip
Measure and then measure again. You don't want to do all this work, only to paint your design crooked or off-center! Trust me, I've done it. Then your lovely bridal tee turns into a pajama tee.

4 Paint Design Insert a piece of cardboard or similar thick material between the shirt front and back. Using a foam brush with a small amount of paint, start going over the design. The freezer paper should minimize any paint bleed-through, but it is better to opt for multiple thin paint coats over laying on a thick paint coat. I chose to leave my letters rough and worn looking, but a second and third light coat will cover the area. Before the paint dries completely, slowly pull away the freezer paper.

ask your

bridesmaids

[monogrammed calendar] *So She Doesn't Miss A Thing*

This gift is as much for you as it is for her. It will be a lovely place for your bridesmaid to keep all the dates and details of your wedding so she doesn't miss a thing.

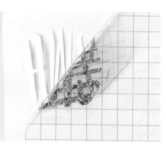

Supplies

- Pocket calendar
- Self-adhesive holographic vinyl (available near the electronic cutting machines)
- Transfer tape for vinyl (available near the electronic cutting machines)

Tools

- Computer and printer
- Scissors
- Heavy-duty detail craft knife
- Ruler
- Tape
- Self-healing cutting mat

STEPS

1 Create Monogram In Word, or a comparable application, select your favorite font. Place your bridesmaid's last name initial in the center and flank the sides with the first and middle name initials. Make the two outer letters slightly smaller than the center letter. Measure the calendar and size the group to fit on the calendar. Print the template.

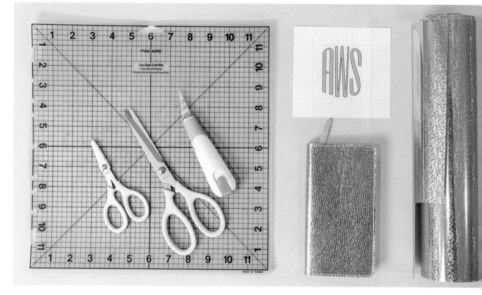

ask your

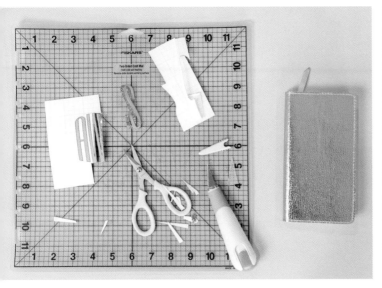

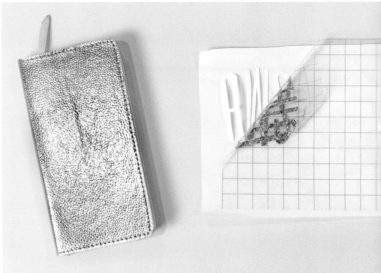

2 Cut Place the template on a piece of holographic vinyl. Tape together along the edges. Using scissors and a heavy duty craft knife for small areas, cut out the design, carefully removing the excess material.

3 Transfer Using a small piece of transfer tape, peel the vinyl from its backer.

4 Place Measure the calendar to find the center point and using the guides on the transfer tape, adhere the monogram on the calendar.

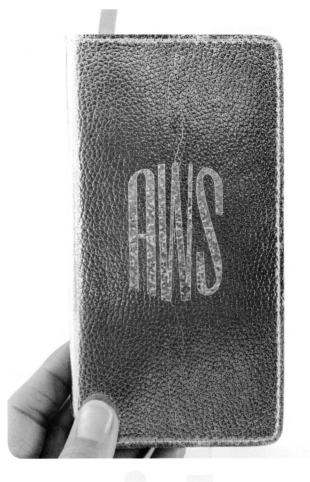

bridesmaids

[bridesmaid gift box]
Packaging Made Perfect

An invitation is exciting, but take it a step further and spoil her. Tell her you appreciate her and that you're excited for her to be a part of your big day with a beautiful gift box full of wedding essentials: bridesmaid tee, "flawless" makeup bag, monogrammed calendar and of course, chocolate!

Supplies

- Box, either cardboard or wood
- Decorative-edge, colored tissue paper
- Gift box filler
- Bow
- Bridesmaid T-shirt
- Makeup bag
- Wrapped chocolates
- Monogrammed calendar (see page 24)
- Invitation (see page 18)

STEPS

1 Gather Supplies This craft is all about color coordination, space management and buying pretty. You want your colors to work together, but they don't have to be matchy-matchy. Choose most of your items and then choose your box. You want them all to fit well. And of course, always buy gifts for your friends that you yourself would want.

2 Organize & Pack Layer the tissue paper in the bottom of the box, fill with gift box filler and start laying in your gifts, placing the heaviest at the bottom. Place the invitation and chocolates on top!

Don't kid yourself; packaging is important. It builds excitement and tells your bridesmaid that you put more than 10 minutes of thought into her gift. She'll be spending hours and even days with you over the next several months; make sure she knows she's loved right from the beginning!

26

ask your bride

say i do

Delight in the Details

Little touches on your big day will make the
sweetest memories!

The memories are in the making, of crafts that is! Dig into the fine details
of your wedding day and personalize all that you can. Make yourself a
special hanger for your wedding dress, host a memorable brunch for your
bridesmaids. Plan ahead and do all the things you've dreamed about.
Then give a list of your handmade creations to your photographer so
they don't miss a thing about your handmade day!

[bride hanger]
You Found The Perfect Dress

This craft is worth the effort! And, will help make your dress photos perfect. Plus, let's face it, it's just plain pretty. You can make something darling like this "bride" hanger, or use this same technique to spell out your new last name!

Supplies

- 15 to 20 gauge wire
- Wooden hanger

Tools

- Computer and printer
- Wire cutters
- Round-nose pliers
- Finishing nails
- Hammer
- Small piece of scrap wood
- Ruler

STEPS

1 Gather Supplies Choose bronze, silver or black wire. 20 gauge is lighter and easier to work with, but shows imperfections quicker. 15 gauge is thicker, but gives a more polished look.

2 Measure & Print Name Measure your hanger. Type your name, bride, groom, etc. in your favorite font, size to fit your hanger and print.

tip
Whimsy fonts are more difficult to create with wire. Choose a font with clean and simple flourishes, if any at all.

3 Place & Nail Place the template on the piece of wood and nail a small finishing nail at each curve or angle.

4 Bend Start the wire 2-3 inches from the end; this will allow you to attach the wire to the hanger. Bend and loop the wire over the nails. Take your time. Bending too quickly can cause kinks.

30

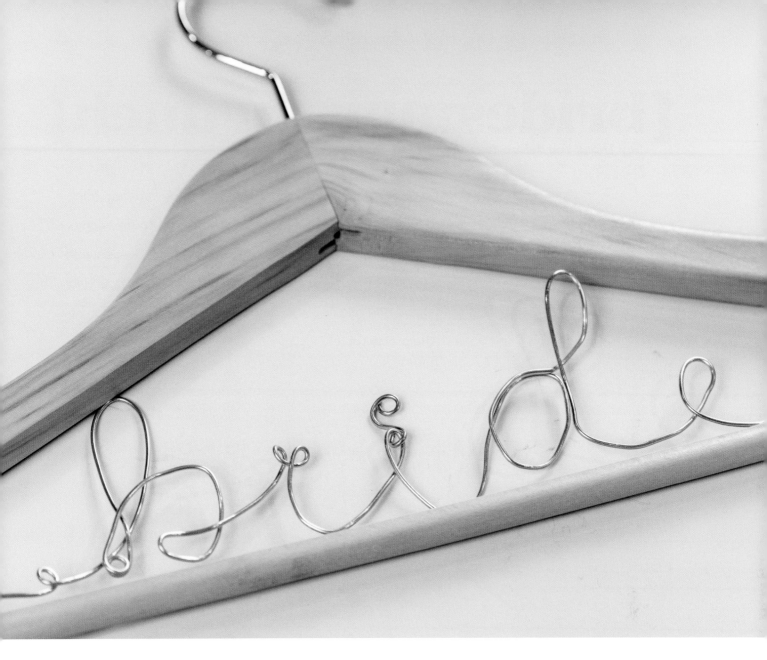

5 Remove From Nails
Carefully remove the wire from the nails. Using pliers, finish and smooth the bends and curves. Lay the wire on a hard surface and flatten with the hammer.

6 Hang Carefully wrap the ends of the wire over the hanger, tuck in the ends and you're ready to use.

Do not pull the wire so tight when you're working with it that you cannot get the wire over the nail heads when removing it. You will add curves and close gaps once the wire is off the template and nails.

say i do

[bridesmaid brunch]

Say Thank You Before You're Swept Off Your Feet

Host a bridesmaid brunch the day before your wedding. Mine was a wonderful opportunity to say thank you to my friends and to get a little encouragement from them. Yes, I was super nervous! The brunch is as easy as setting a pretty table, serving great food and relaxing with amazing friends. Let me help you with the pretty table!

www.leisurearts.com

Use Coordinating Stationery

There are so many pretty stationery items available today – place card mini banners, small signs, thank you tent cards. If you own an electronic cutting machine, you can find many wedding images and shapes that can be personalized. Choose the images and add names or initials to create sweet coordinates for the Bridesmaid Brunch.

For this table I persoanlized place cards, thank you cards and centerpiece signs.

[glass markers]

Supplies

- Pink or coordinating color cardstock
- Hot pink pen or marker

Tools

- Straight edge paper cutter
- Small detail scissors

STEPS

1 Gather Supplies Choose a coordinating color cardstock for the drink markers.

2 Cut Strips Using a straight edge cutter, cut a ¾" x 6" strip for each glass. Notch a triangle out of each end. Cut a half slit 2⅛" from each end, cutting from the top for one slit and from the bottom for the other.

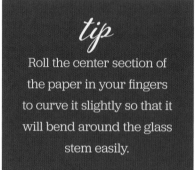

tip

Roll the center section of the paper in your fingers to curve it slightly so that it will bend around the glass stem easily.

3 Personalize Write the name on the strip. Wrap the marker around the glass stem.

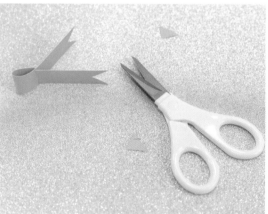

say i do

How To Set The Table – Layer it! This place setting uses a coordinating place mat, paper doily (slightly larger than your dinner plate), dinner plate, fabric napkin, salad plate, and is topped with a ramekin for sweets and place card!

[marbled canning jar vase]

*Give Canning Jar Vases
A Modern Update*

Canning jar vases can be beautifully decorated with ribbon,

but consider painting and marbling them for a modern twist.

Supplies

- Fresh roses in coordinating colors
- Wide mouth canning jar
- White acrylic paint
- Coordinating colors of fingernail polish
- Paper plate
- Water
- Ribbon

Tools

- Disposable aluminum pan
- Wooden skewer

STEPS

1 Gather Supplies Choose nail polish in your wedding colors. I chose three pinks, but test the mixing of complementary colors too, like maybe pink and gold.

2 Paint Paint the interior of the canning jar white by pouring paint in, turning the jar upside down and allowing the paint to drip down the sides onto a paper plate. Once the paint stops dripping, move it to a new plate to dry overnight.

tip

Save the paint. Fold the paper plate and use it as a funnel to return the excess paint to the bottle.

3 Marble Place an inch of water in the disposable aluminum pan. Place a paper plate next to the pan. Pour one color of fingernail polish into the water and stir with a skewer. Working quickly, dip the jar at an angle into the mixture and roll it around. Don't allow water into the jar.

36

4 Dry Place the jar on a paper plate to dry for at least 15 minutes. For multiple colors, repeat step three, washing out the pan and using new water between each nail polish color.

Work Quickly – The nail polish sets quickly in the water. Pour, dip and remove the jar in 20 seconds or less, otherwise the marbling won't be smooth. The nail polish will start to collect together and string, rather than marble, on the jar.

5 Ribbon & Roses Wrap the jar with a coordinating ribbon (I prefer multiple wraps) and fill with water and roses!

say i do

[photo hoop]
Feature Your Engagement Photos

Show off your life together before the wedding in a beautiful embroidery hoop frame! You could even create a collage of three: one hoop of you as a child, one hoop of your betrothed as a child and one hoop of your wedding engagement or dating years. One or all three hoops would be a darling addition above the honey fund, gift or guest book table.

Supplies

- 22" quilting hoop
- Ribbon
- Photos
- Floral stems
- Adhesive dots
- Command™ product for hanging (optional)

Tools

- Hot glue gun
- Ruler

say i do

38

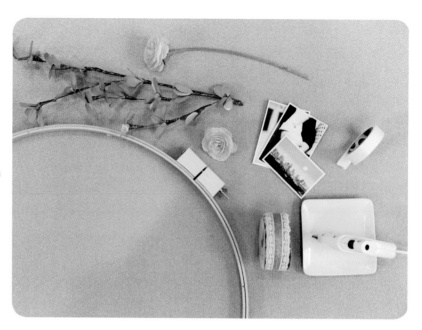

STEPS

1 Gather Supplies For your photos, consider printing them in black and white on cardstock, then trimming them out with a white border so that they look like instant photos.

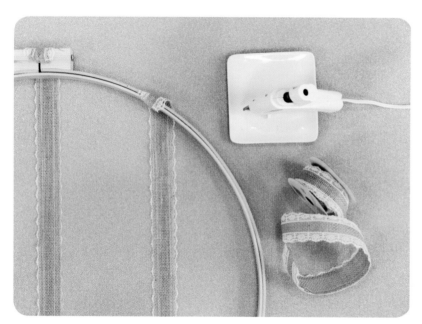

2 Measure & Attach Measure your photos and the width of your hoop to determine how many strips of ribbon you can have. Then, hot glue the ribbon at the hoop top and bottom.

say i do

3 Add Photos Using adhesive dots, attach your photos to the center of the ribbons, leaving space between each photo.

4 Add Florals Using hot glue, attach florals in your wedding colors to the hoop center top. Bend them to curve around the top of the hoop.

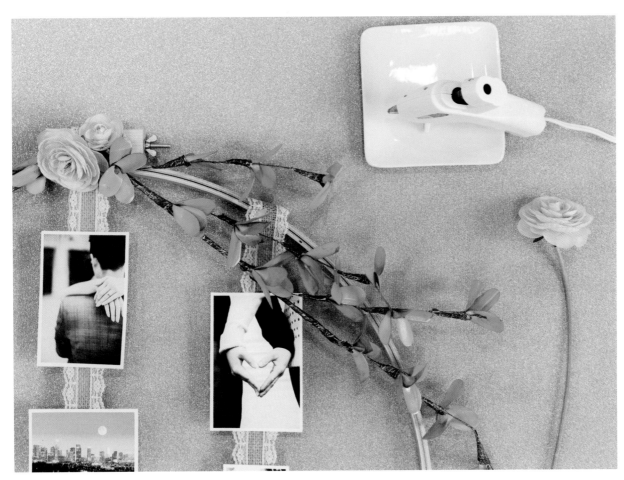

[boutonnieres]
Something For Him

Florals don't have to be intimidating, especially boutonnieres and bouquets. Keep them simple and they're a cinch. Roses are always beautiful and timeless, but if you want to be unique, search for florals in your wedding color palette and don't be afraid to mix them up. It's hard to go wrong!

Supplies

- Florals, at least two elements
- Ribbon
- Straight pins
- Floral tape

Tools

- Floral snips

STEPS

1 Gather Supplies Layering is key when creating boutonnieres, so consider flowers that work well together, but where one is clearly the star. You can keep it simple with two, or you can go more, but remember that you don't want to overpower the lapel.

2 Trim Select your flowers, trim away any stray pieces or anything that looks like it is wilting and start to bundle and arrange them in your fingers.

3 Wrap Using floral tape, wrap the stems from the top of the flower down. Cut off the excess stem.

4 Embellish Add a ribbon bow or wrap ribbon all the way down the stem. You can also use twine or other elements that work well with your wedding theme.

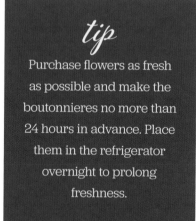

tip

Purchase flowers as fresh as possible and make the boutonnieres no more than 24 hours in advance. Place them in the refrigerator overnight to prolong freshness.

42

Not all boutonnieres are created equal. Make something unique for the groom that coordinates with the rest of the wedding party.

reception
Time to Celebrate

#8

You're married!

Your friends and family just witnessed you giving your life to the man you will love 'til death do you part. Now it's time to pop the bubbly and dance the night away. Make your reception uniquely you and personalize it all, from the table numbers to the wedding favors to the cake topper! Let's party!

[monogram table numbers]

Faux Foil

Place your new last name front and center at your reception tables with a monogram table number card. Take it a step further and create a faux gold foil effect!

This easy craft can be personalized with your favorite font, wedding colors, and sweet sentiments in minutes. It can also be bright and colorful, or elegant and monochromatic. Dress up the cards to have a gold foil look without the expense!

Supplies

- White cardstock
- Metallic gold marker, such as Sharpie™

Tools

- Computer and printer
- Straight edge cutter
- Ruler

reception

table
5

ANGELA & SCOTT
THREE YEARS AND COUNTING

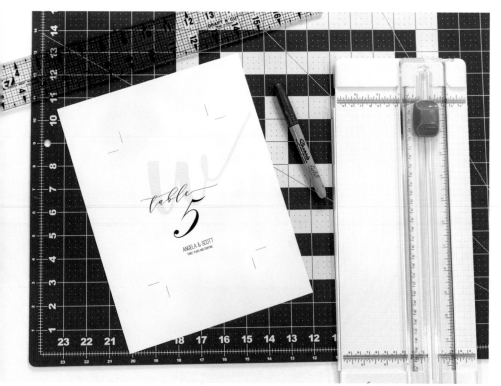

STEPS

1 Gather Supplies Get the look of gold foil, without the expense by using a gold marker to outline your table number. Or leave the card an elegant black and white!

2 Create & Print Layer 1 Simply open a new Word (or comparable application) document, make a text box 4" x 6" (insert>text box), choose a font you like, make it large in the box, turn the color of the font to a light grey (or another color) and print. Print as many cards as you need.

3 Create & Print Layer 2 In the same file, delete the monogram. Center your table number, names and a sentiment in the text box. Overprint onto the same cardstock you just printed and repeat the process for the rest of your table numbers.

4 Make Faux Gold Foil Use a gold marker to draw diagonal lines with a ruler and to fill in your table number.

www.leisurearts.com

5 Cut Use the straight edge cutter to cut out the card.

Add color easily by printing on colored cardstock, or layering a patterned paper (slightly larger so you can see the edges) behind the number card.

tip

Test print the card on plain paper to check the size, color and placement of the monogram and words before printing on cardstock.

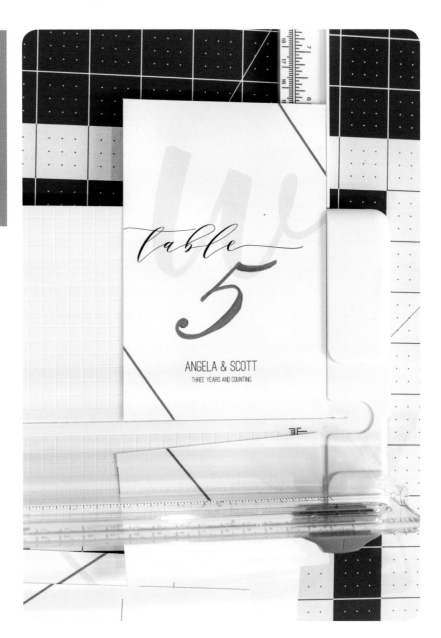

reception

Try Glass Milk Bottles

These are the sweetest elements. Very inexpensive whether you buy them dipped or you paint them yourself. I suggest nesting several with your florals on platters or trays for easy arranging. Plus, you won't have to worry about uneven table runners, like this moss runner, tipping the bottles over.

Vary Heights

Consider varying the height of the items in your centerpiece. The different elevations bring interest to the table, and allows you more flexibility in what you can add to the mix. For instance, I wanted to use, my table number easel, but then felt it was lost – too low to the table. By adding a small footed cake plate for

Remember, this wedding is about you and your groom. If you have a limited budget, focus on the most photographed table, your own. Guest tables can still be beautiful, just be smart about your choices and craft!

tip

When using white dishware and cake plates, whether your own or rented, they can get boring. Liven them up with your wedding's color palette. For pennies, you can trim cardstock to fit inside the rim!

the easel, I raised it up and put the table number back in view from around the room!

Consider Greenery

Fabric is beautiful, but not always easy especially when you can't find your color or a pattern that works for your special day. Consider using greenery instead. If you're celebrating with a tropical themed wedding, use large palms to make a natural runner. Or in this table's case, use a moss runner. It comes in a roll and you only trim off what you need.

reception

[place setting ideas]

Consider A Seasonal Table

Place settings can be as complex or as simple as you want. No matter what you choose, I have one suggestion. Don't only assign people to tables, but assign them to seats. Place cards can be your best friend when you don't want Aunt Martha sitting next to Cousin Craig. Plus, they can be darling too!

Don't only assign people to tables, but assign them to seats.

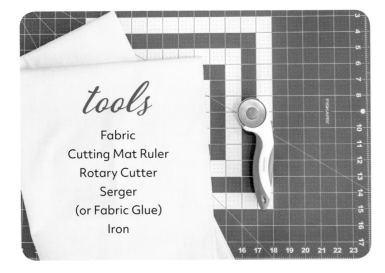

tools

Fabric
Cutting Mat Ruler
Rotary Cutter
Serger
(or Fabric Glue)
Iron

Linens

It's easy to rent white linens, but if you want to punch up the color, make your own! It can be as simple as fabric, thread and a serger. Or, if you don't have a serger, use an iron for perfect hems and finish with fabric glue. Either way, you'll have perfectly matched linens!

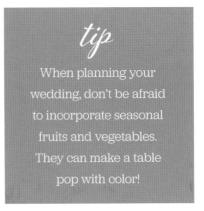

tip

When planning your wedding, don't be afraid to incorporate seasonal fruits and vegetables. They can make a table pop with color!

[easel table numbers]

Make Seating Guests Easy & Creative

Table numbers are simple crafts, but they can be as unique or creative as you want. These tiny easels are perfect for most any reception style. Paint them, chalk them, embellish them, stencil them, add florals to them – your imagination is your only limit.

Supplies

- Reversible mini easels (chalkboard side and white board side)
- Paint in a wide mouth container large enough to dip the mini easels into
- Foam paintbrush
- Number stencils or number stickers (cardboard, glitter or foil)
- Chalk marker if stenciling
- Tape
- Small dowels

reception

52

STEPS

1 Gather Supplies This craft works for all kinds of things. Just make sure the item you want to dip will fit in your paint can opening, or you have a larger container to transfer the paint into. Also, make clean-up easy on yourself with cardboard or a poster board to cover the work surface.

2 Dip Mix the paint very well with a paint stir stick or a wooden dowel. Dip the easel and hold it over the paint can for 10-15 seconds so the excess drips off.

reception

3 Dry Place the dipped easel on dowels so that the paint doesn't puddle on the bottom. Allow to dry completely overnight.

4 Embellish Tape a stencil to the easel and use a chalk marker to paint the number on the easel front and back. Or, center and adhere number stickers on the front and back. It's that easy!

tip

Be attentive – Rotate the easel multiple times during the drying process so that there are no "think" paint areas on the bottom.

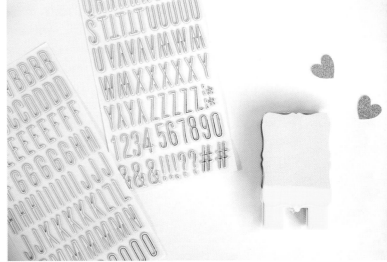

[matchbox covers]
You're a perfect match!

Every wedding couple needs their own personalized matchbox! These affordable and handy keepsakes are a classic. They're not only perfect for lighting the candles at the reception, but guests tend to pocket them because they're so practical.

Supplies

- Black chalkboard cardstock
- Matchboxes
- Adhesive dots

Tools

- Straight edge cutter
- White chalk marker
- Phrase and alphabet stamps

STEPS

1 Gather Supplies Look for small stamps and alphabet sets, no larger than 2" x 1½".

2 Cut Using a straight edge cutter, cut 2" x 1 ½" cardstock rectangles. You'll need two for each matchbox.

3 Chalk & Stamp Using a chalk marker, paint the stamp quickly and center on paper. Press firmly and lift the stamp straight up. Allow chalk ink to dry for 30 seconds before handling or you risk smudging the ink.

4 Assemble Using glue dots, place a sentiment on one side of the matchbook and the bride and groom's initials on the opposite side.

www.leisurearts.com

Place these keepsakes on each table at your reception. Perfect for lighting candles!

[succulent favors]

Sow the seeds of love with favors that guests won't leave behind!

Guests will love these small succulents. Nestle them in white or terracotta pots, dip them in your wedding colors and let them double as both favor and table number!

Supplies

- Mini flower pots
- Small succulent plants
- Sphagnum moss
- Green peat moss

- Paint in a wide mouth container large enough to dip the mini pots into
- Wooden dowels

STEPS

1 Gather Supplies

Succulents are easy to handle, won't wilt and barely need any water. Plus, there is no need for potting soil. The small amount that comes with the root ball is more than enough.

tip

Pots should be just slightly larger than the plant root ball.

No Potting Soil Needed!

58

tip

Be attentive - rotate
the pot multiple times
during the drying
process so that there
are no "thick" paint
areas on the bottom.

2 Plant Wrap each plant in sphagnum moss. It's a long fibered moss that is essential for soilless planting. Place a very small amount of water, no more than a teaspoon, on each root ball and plant in the mini pots. Decorate the top of the planter with peat moss.

3 Dip Mix the paint very well with a paint stir stick or a wooden dowel. Dip the pot into the paint at a angle and hold it over the paint can for 10-15 seconds so the excess drips off.

4 Dry Place the pots on dowels so that the paint doesn't puddle on the bottom. Allow to dry completely, usually overnight.

reception

[mini pennant table numbers]

Place Card & Wedding Favor In One

Supplies

- Kraft cardstock
- Thin wooden dowels

Tools

- Pennant punch or scissors
- Hole punch that will accomodate dowel
- Fine-tip marker or pen

STEPS

1 Make Use a small pennant punch to make small flags. If you prefer to use scissors, make a template of a pennant shape and then use it as a guide to cut out the flags.

2 Punch Punch two small holes for the dowel (test before you punch all the pennants).

3 Write Place guest name and table number on each pennant.

4 Insert Thread pennant onto a dowel. Add a pennant to each succulent favor.

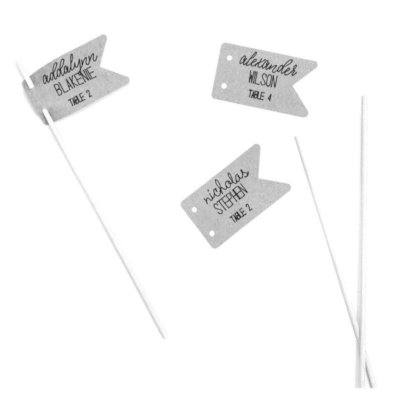

60

reception

[mr. & mrs. chair backs]

Mark Your Spot

Let all your guests know where you'll be during dinner with these darling chair back signs. Personalize them to your color palette with florals like I did, or another element that ties them to your wedding style!

Supplies

- Chalkboard signs, about 6" x 9"
- Cardstock
- White chalk marker
- Floral stems

Tools

- Ruler
- Craft knife
- Painter's tape
- Self-healing mat
- Hot glue gun

STEPS

1 Gather Supplies Live florals are beautiful and a great way to go if your florist will be embellishing the signs for you. Or, choose lifelike silk flowers that you can arrange and hot glue to the back of your signs in advance. In either case, select greenery and a large bloom to achieve this look. Or you can bundle greenery and several small blooms. Make it your own!

reception

2 Copy & Cut Photocopy Mr. and Mrs. templates (pages 90-91) onto cardstock. Using a craft knife, trim the letters out of the cardstock, creating a stencil. Trim off the excess white area around the word as well, so that you can easily center it on the sign.

3 Chalk Tape the stencil to a sign. Using a chalk marker, start by outlining within the stencil. Make sure that you use the cutout portions within the loop letters too. Once you have a good outline, remove the template and start filling in the letters with strokes all going in one direction.

4 Embellish If you're adding silk florals, cut to desired length and hot glue to the back of the sign. Make sure they don't obscure your letters!

Clean-up Tip – If you mess up, go outside the lines or smudge the chalk, just grab a small paintbrush, a small bowl of water and a paper towel. Use the paintbrush to lightly wet the area and the paper towel to soak it up. Dab, don't wipe.

[cake topper]
To Top It Off

One of the most photographed items at your wedding will be the cake! Make it dreamy with a custom cake topper you've made yourself. It could be a whimsical phrase like "Happily Ever After," "Forever Yours" or create a special sentiment that only you and your new husband share!

Supplies

- Mat board
- Thin wooden dowel
- Spray paint (wedding color and glitter)
- White cardstock
- Tape

Tools

- Heavy-duty craft knife
- Self-healing cutting mat
- Hot glue gun

STEPS

1 Gather Supplies
Photocopy Happily Ever After template (page 92) onto cardstock.

2 Cut Trim off the excess cardstock around the print. Tape it to the front of the mat board. Using a heavy-duty craft knife, cut out the design on a self-healing cutting mat. I recommend taking your time and going over the design multiple times instead of trying to cut too deep on the first pass. This will help keep the edges and lines smooth.

66

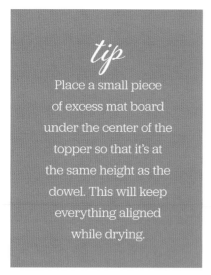

tip

Place a small piece of excess mat board under the center of the topper so that it's at the same height as the dowel. This will keep everything aligned while drying.

3 Paint Add a bit of color with spray paint. My best advice is to move from side to side swiftly from a few feet away. Paint in multiple coats and angles, allowing the paint to get into small grooves and around edges. Take your time. Allow the topper to dry for at least two hours before applying the glitter spray paint coat. Then allow the topper to dry for at least two more hours before attaching the dowel.

Only paint in a well ventilated area, preferably outside weather permitting. Painting outside below 55 degrees will affect adhesion, the paint will be tacky, and refuse to dry. As much as you might want to, don't try it. Go to plan B and use a small brush and craft paint if you're running low on time.

4 Attach Dowel Flip the topper over and measure to find the center point. Add a small amount of hot glue and place the dowel.

reception

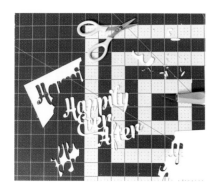

68

Before placing your cake topper, use another dowel and a ruler to find the center point of your cake, measuring from all four sides. Place a small indention in the icing to mark your spot and you'll have a perfectly centered cake topper every time.

tip

Choose someone you trust to add florals to your cake an hour or so before your reception. The florals should be removed from water, dried thoroughly with a paper towel, excess stems trimmed away and placed gently atop the cake or cake plate. Caution! Some flowers are poisonous. Discuss options with your florist and bakery.

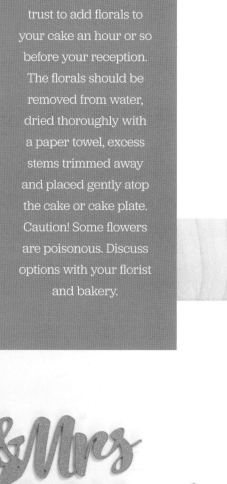

[guest book]
Think Beyond The Book

Instead of a traditional guest book that you'll likely store away, have your guests leave their wit, charm and love on stones that you can display in your new home. They'll be a lovely reminder of the love and well wishes you received on your big day!

Supplies

- Smooth black stones
- Fine-point paint pens
- White cardstock
- Glass vessels to hold blank and signed stones
- Wood pallet-style sign
- Glue dots
- Spray paint (if you can't find black stones)

Tools

- Straight edge cutter

STEPS

1 Gather Supplies If you can't locate black stones, purchase any color and spray paint them.

2 Copy & Cut Photocopy the guest book sign (page 93) onto white cardstock. Trim the sign if necessary using the straight edge paper cutter. Attach the sign to a wood pallet sign with glue dots.

3 Lead By Example To show guests what to do, have your wedding party sign the stones at the rehearsal dinner and place them in the glass vessels before the first guests arrive. This not only gives guests guidance, but it allows those closest to you time to participate. They'll be a little preoccupied on the big day!

4 Decorate Make the area inviting and interesting so guests don't pass right by. Display the guest book sign on a pallet-style sign as I did or in a 8x10 picture frame. Add florals to the table along with a bold coordinating ribbon.

70

tip

My best advice for painiting is to take your time, moving from side to side swiftly and painting from every angle to get down into small grooves and around the edges. This process may require a few days. You'll need to paint one side of the stones on a flat surface (e.g., cardboard), allow the stones to dry completely, flip and paint the other side. Most likely, two coats will be needed.

Only paint in a well ventilated area, preferably outside weather permitting. Painting outside below 55 degrees will affect adhesion, the paint will be tacky, and refuse to dry. As much as you might want to, don't try it. Go to plan B and use a small brush and craft paint.

[honey fund frame]

Honeymoon Gifts Are A Thing

Make a Honey Fund frame for your reception. It's a great way for family and friends to contribute to your honeymoon. I know we had several family members that wanted to buy us dinner while we were away or give us a spa visit. It was so very sweet and this allows those loving family members to do that for you!

Supplies

- Top-loading clear picture frame
- Destination photo
- Alpahbet, heart and "Thank You" stickers
- Glue dots

Tools

- Ruler

STEPS

1 Gather Supplies Make this project your own and customize it to your honeymoon destination with a photo.

reception

2 Measure & Attach Inside Measure your clear frame back and adhere the honeymoon destination photo with glue dots. It will be on the inside of the frame.

3 Measure, Peel & Attach Outside Measure the front of the frame, arrange the letter stickers, peel away the backings and adhere stickers to top glass.

3 Add Sentiment Say thank you for their generosity with heart and thank you stickers.

reception

[mr. & mrs.
Calling All Coffee And Tea Lovers!
personalized mugs]

Surprise your better half-to-be with personalized mugs. Each morning as you start a new day together, you'll remember the blessed day that started it all!

Supplies

- Ceramic coffee mugs
- White rectangular label stickers
- Permanent markers, such as Sharpie®

Tools

- Craft knife
- Self-healing mat
- Baking sheet

STEPS

1 Gather Supplies Choose pens that match your wedding colors, or chose a classic gold or silver. Photocopy the templates on page 94.

2 Slice Place each template over a rectangular sticker and "draw" through the center of each letter with the craft knife. This will make a thin slit down the center of each letter.

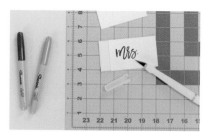

3 Paint/Draw Place the sticker on the mug. Use the marker to draw the letters on the mug through the letter slits. Faint lines of the letters will be on the mug. Remove the sticker and draw over the letters on the mug. Add any additional personalization.

4 Clean-Up If done quickly, you can clean up the lettering using a damp cloth and medium pressure. For small areas, wrap the cloth around the edge of the craft knife.

5 Bake Place your mugs on a baking sheet; place the baking sheet into a cold oven. Heat the oven to 350 degrees and bake the mugs for 30 minutes. This will set the ink. I recommend hand washing the mugs.

reception

76

Messed up? No worries! Use a damp cloth to remove the design or lettering and try again!

just married

mrs.

JEWELL

blow bubbles

OF WELL WISHES FOR THE NEW Mr. & Mrs.

send off

Your Honeymoon Is Waiting

Let the guests join in the fun to
send you off with fanfare!

Whether it's bubbles or bells, guests need a way to say goodbye, wish
you luck and gather those last hugs. Farewells can sometimes last for
what feels like forever, but the last laughs and tears will be some of
your most precious memories as you start your new life as a Mrs!.

[bubble wands]
Beautiful Bubbles

Bubbles are a great way for everyone to get involved in your send off. They're inexpensive, fun, no clean up, and best of all, darling in photos!

Supplies

- Papier-mâché hat box
- Burlap and lace ribbons (one wide, one narrower)
- Bubble wands
- ½" wide ribbon for bubble wands
- Gift box filler
- White cardstock
- Wooden paddle
- Adhesive dots

Supplies

- Hot glue gun
- Small detail scissors

STEPS

1 Gather Supplies Choose a hat box and coordinating ribbons. You'll want a wide ribbon for the box and a more narrow ribbon for the lip of the lid. You'll also want a small ½" wide ribbon for the bubble wands.

2 Embellish Hat Box Using hot glue, attach the wide ribbon to the side of the box all the way around.

3 Make Sign Photocopy the sign (page 95) onto cardstock. Cut out the sign using the small detail scissors. Attach the sign to a wooden paddle with adhesive dots.

Want your sign to be a color? Photocopy the design onto colored cardstock!

4 Embellish Add ribbon to each wand to dress them up a bit and coordinate with your wedding colors. Fill the hat box with gift box filler. Nestle the wands in the filler, standing them up. Add the sign to the back of the box.

80

[tambourines]
A Chorus Of Bells

How pretty are these tulle and hoop tambourines? This craft is easy to make and is a fun keepsake for your guests. Consider gathering your bridesmaids for a crafty tambourine-making party (it never hurts to ask for help!). It's so easy you won't even need a needle. A little bubbly, tambourine supplies and lots of wedding talk make for a festive affair!

Supplies
(for one tambourine)

- ⅓ yard tulle (at least 52" wide)
- 14 jingle bells, about ½" diameter
- 6" wooden embroidery hoop
- Ribbon
- Clear fishing line

(for baskets)

- Small wire baskets
- White cardstock
- Adhesive dots

Tools

- Hot glue gun
- Ruler
- Scissors
- Detail scissors

STEPS

1 Gather Supplies I chose to make 6" tambourines, but mini 4" hoops would be darling too and more economical if you have a large guest list. These are often made with lace. They're lovely, but tulle is so beautiful; it shimmers in the light and is a fraction of the price.

Gone are the days of bird seed. Now, brides are loving bubbles, sparklers and tambourines. All pretty and all environmentally safe!

2 Fold, Hoop & Hot Glue
Matching the short ends, fold the tulle in fourths and place in the hoop. There should be an excess of about 2"-3" on all sides. With sharp scissors, trim off the excess all the way around. Hot glue ribbon around the hoop outer edge.

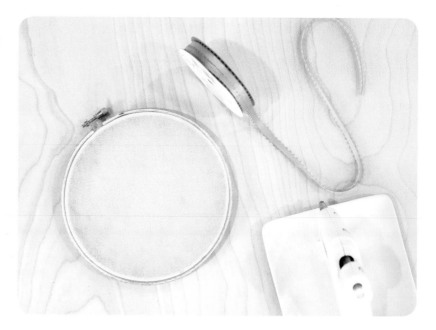

3 Tie Bells Cut a 36" length of fishing line. Tie the line to the hoop near the screwpin. Thread the line through the tulle and slide on a bell. Wrap the line around the hoop and come back through the tulle about 1¼" from the bell and slide on another bell. Continue to add the remaining bells in the same manner. Tie off the line. You can use a drop of hot glue on the underside of the hoop rim after each bell so that the line doesn't slip and the bells don't move.

send off

4 Embellish Add a sweet little bow to the top of the hoop, hiding the closure. You could also personalize your tambourines with a monogram or the initials of you and your betrothed. Hand stitching on tulle is almost effortless.

5 Arrange Buy small wire baskets and place the tambourines all around your reception for a romantic jingle bell send off! Photocopy the sign (page 94) onto white cardstock and use detail scissors to cut out. Make one for each basket. Use adhesive dots to attach the signs to the wire baskets.

PLEASE
take AND *shake*

templates

#BRIDE TRIBE

He
popped

the
question!

Will you help me tie the knot?

Happily Ever After

Guest Book

please
sign a stone

and be a
light unto our path
with your
witt, charm, & love

Mr. Mrs.

PLEASE
take AND *shake*

blow
bubbles

OF WELL WISHES

FOR THE NEW

Mr. & Mrs.

kim wilson byers

Kim Wilson Byers is the creative director & owner of The Celebration Shoppe, a graphic design studio and lifestyle blog at TheCelebrationShoppe.com . Kim shares crafts, entertaining ideas and recipes with thousands of readers every day.

Kim has been blessed to have her designs, party ideas and recipes featured in a number of nationally published magazines including Parents, Better Homes and Gardens, All You and Pregnancy, to name just a few.

In addition to sharing creative and easy craft tutorials with her readers, Kim also designs paper crafts for select craft companies and has her own line of party crafts and cake kits available on Amazon and Etsy.

Kim lives on 20 acres nestled in the rolling hills at the tip of the Appalachian Mountain range in Alabama with her husband of 20 years and her two sons.

Kim has her Master's degree in Marketing and spent the first 10 years of her career in investment management, only to have her complete perspective on what's important change in an instant when her boys were born. Kim still works more hours than is often reasonable, but from her home studio where being a mom can take precedence anytime she's needed.

Kim Wilson Byers, crafter, entertaining expert and graphic designer, shows thousands of readers every day tips and ideas on how to make the big and small moments personal and memorable.

Kim also designs paper crafts for cartridges for Cricut® cutting machines; find them at TheCelebrationShoppe.com/CricutCartridges

Made in U.S.A.

Library of Congress Control Number: 2018945347

Photography by Kim Byers. Some additional images used by license from Shutterstock.com.

We have made every effort to ensure that these instructions are accurate and complete. We cannot, however, be responsible for human error, typographical mistakes, or variations in individual work.

Production Team: Technical Editor – Mary Sullivan Hutcheson; Graphic Designer – Kate Lanphier.